Proverbs for Kids
and those who love them

Volume 2

How God Teaches
Wisdom Using

parts of the human body

Robert M. Gullberg

My Proverbs Study Book

Presented to:_____
By:_____
Date:_____

Proverbs for Kids- Proverbs for Kids- Ten Volume Series:

    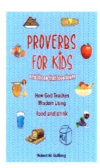

  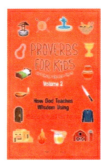  

Written by Robert M. Gullberg M.D. Print and E-book versions found at **www.proverbsforkidsamazon.com**
All rights reserved. No part of this publication may be reproduced in any form without written
permission from In House Faith Publishing at rgullberg@wi.rr.com

Printed in the United States of America

Acknowledgements: All Scripture verses taken from the *NIV (New International Version) Bible*, *Living Bible*, or *The Message* (Public Domain). All images are free and not copyrighted. Teachable Truths come from numerous internet sources. Cover Art: Shad Smith. Thanks to John R. Gullberg, Laurie Stecher, and Jim Magruder for editorial assistance.

Contents

A Word from the Author..4

Arms- Learn to *help the less fortunate person* with
"open arms"..6

Bones- *Having a joyful attitude* will help your health.
Being sad leads to problems with physical one's well-being...................11

Ears- Learn to be a good listener. *Hear the Word of
God as much as you can* and apply it to your life.....................................16

Face- *Treat others like you want to be treated*. Be
compassionate to others..20

Fingers- Commit to knowing God's principles *so that your
mind will change* and you will be a new person......................................25

Head- Learn to *love your enemy as you love yourself*.
Who is your enemy? 30

Stomach- Learn to *be thankful for what God has given
you*. Fill your heart with his Spirit and you will always
be satisfied...35

Teeth- Learn to *be a faithful friend* and more fully
committed to God...39

Following God..44

Proverbs in this Book..45

Principles Taught in this Book...45

A Word from the Author

Proverbs for Kids -Volume 2

Ever wonder how God talks to kids?

God is the greatest storyteller, and throughout the Bible he uses creative and inspiring ways to help us learn Biblical truths. He often uses the "things of this world" such as clouds, the sun, oceans, darkness, deserts, light, the wind, water, earthly creatures, parts of the human body, and everyday things around the house (to name a few!) to teach us eternal truths. In the Old Testament, God teaches us his timeless wisdom from the Book of Proverbs. In the New Testament, Jesus tells numerous stories, called parables, to help teach deep spiritual lessons. He uses common concepts such as farming, money, fig trees, soil, doors, and fishing to teach important life lessons. The practical teachings contained in Proverbs were inspired by God and given to mankind over 2,000 years ago. The book was written around 920 B.C. primarily by King Solomon. According to the Bible, he was the wisest man who has ever lived. While 920 B.C. was a long time ago, his teaching principles still hold true for today!

Proverbs for Kids- Volume 2 is a continuation of a series of ten inspirational books covering over 90 proverbs designed to teach children Biblical truths in a fun, easy, and entertaining way. These concepts captivate the imagination and help kids understand important truths in a language they can understand. What is more is both kids and adults who read to them will enjoy these informative and colorful books. The books are especially good for kids between 5 and 11 years of age. This volume in the series shows how God uses **parts of the human body** to help explain foundational spiritual truths. As a medical doctor, I am especially interested in our bodies and how they work. When we look at the wonder of our bodies, we see the hand of an incredible Inventor- God himself. **Psalms 139:13-14** says: "For you God created my inmost being; you knit me together in my mother's womb. I praise you because I am fearfully and wonderfully made; your works are wonderful, and I know that full well." The other books in this series are about **things around the house, earthly creatures, food and drink,** and **things in nature**.

Each of the books in the series contain **Teachable Truths** and the **Take Home**

Points to explain the proverb(s) in more detail. There are **Other Key Verses** from the Bible to reinforce the point of the proverb. Many of these verses of scripture serve as great memory verses and they are contained at the end of each section.

The **Conclusion** at the end of each topic reinforces the *main point* of the Proverb to make memorable teaching. The eight books in the *Proverbs for Kids* series are easy to navigate with enlarged pictures that accompany the associated Proverbs. The *Proverbs for Kids* book series coupled with the time you invest reading to your kids or grandchildren will engrain Biblical wisdom they can draw on for the rest of their lives! With so many difficult challenges we face to raise godly children in today's upside-down culture, it is important to introduce them from a young age to God who loves them dearly. Learning about God together is the right way to go and will enhance our family relationships even more.

As you read through Proverbs for Kids, you will be able to picture yourself growing up in Israel during Bible times to see how God used *parts of the human body* to teach us his wisdom. That wisdom is the same today as it was yesterday. May God use this book to draw many young hearts and minds toward understanding spiritual truth and right ways of living. I hope this inspirational book will be a great adventure for your family.

-Robert M. Gullberg

If you have a quick moment, it would mean a lot if you could go to your "orders" page on Amazon to leave a review for this book. Thank you.

Comments on the Proverbs for Kids series:
Sullivan Bell, 7 years old, said "I love the drawings and the stories."
Sawyer Bell, 8-1/2 years old, said "I like the books because they teach me about God and his wisdom."
Brooklyn Bell, 11 years old, said "It is a good learning experience for me because I like studying with my grandpa."
Jack Bell (grandpa), *Navigators Representative, professional Life and Leadership Coach, said* "It has been fun teaching God's truth from Proverbs for Kids. It has created a whole new spiritual dimension with me and my grandchildren. It fulfills Deuteronomy 4:9 and 6:7--*"God tells us to impress his commandments on our children and their children after them and to talk about them when we sit at home and when we walk along the road, when we lie down and when we get up."*

Arms

Having outstretched arms is a good way to live your life

Teachable Truths:

Human arms are attached to the body at the shoulder joints and give us the ability to pull, throw, hug, and push away. The hands are attached to the arms at the wrist joints. With our hands and fingers, we can also grip and squeeze objects. The upper arms have powerful muscles called biceps and triceps muscles. The large, rounded, and strong muscle on the shoulder allows us to lift the arm up sideways. The elbow is a large hinge joint about halfway down the arm which enables us to use

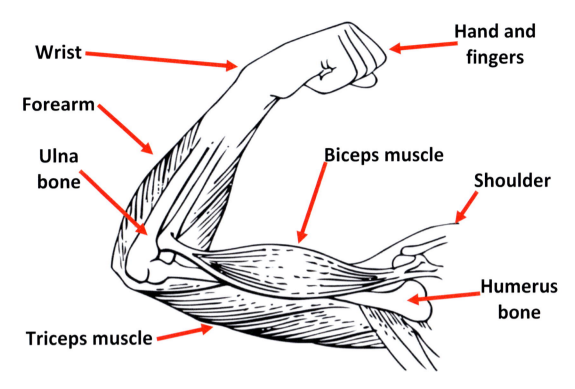

Color the muscles red, the bones white, and the skin your color

leverage as we push and pull objects towards us or away from us. Our elbow allows us to rotate our hand and forearm by more than 180 degrees. There are three main nerves from the cervical (neck) spinal cord that go down each arm all the way to the fingertips. There is one major artery (called the brachial artery) that goes down each arm through the shoulder and it has many important branches.

Verse to review:
Proverbs 31:20 She (the wife of noble character) opens her **arms** to the poor and extends her hands to the needy.

Take Home Points:

This proverb speaks of the wife who has noble and upright character. Noble means having honor, being good, and putting others ahead of yourself. The characteristics of the wife (and mother perhaps) that stand out here are: 1) her hard work 2) her physical strength to finish tasks and 3) her care for those who are in need.

This mother has a business and takes care of her daughter

We can extend this proverb for all people (not just mothers), including kids. Remember our great role model is God himself. He gives to us his strength *and* grace (free kindness) by his outstretched arms (read **Exodus 6:6**, **Psalm 136:12**) so we are to do the same. One of the gifts God can give us is called "helps." (read **1 Corinthians 12:28**) This gift is key for the Christian. Our arms are gifts from God that help us to do God's mission on earth which is to help other people. Learn to do what Jesus did by reading about him the Gospels (Matthew, Mark, Luke, or John). Remember that Jesus IS God. God loves it when you act like Jesus.

The gift of "helps" requires a humble attitude and able arms to carry out the tasks at hand. This could be helping a neighbor mow their lawn or shovel their driveway. It could also mean helping a fellow student with homework who is struggling. Lastly, we should remember the "down and outer." We want to be compassionate to the needs of others. We take care of the poor when they need help. We look after the "have nots" of the world.

You can help a neighbor shovel their sidewalk after a snow storm

Doing things that help others requires able arms!

Other key verses:

Exodus 6:6 The Lord said, "I will bring you out from under the Egyptians. I will free you from being their slaves, and I will redeem you with an outstretched arm and with mighty acts of judgment."

Psalm 136:12 With the Lord's mighty hand and outstretched arm; his love endures (continues) forever.

1 Corinthians 12:28 God has appointed those have been given many gifts including the gift of "helps".

Conclusion: Learn to help the less fortunate person with "open arms."

Bones

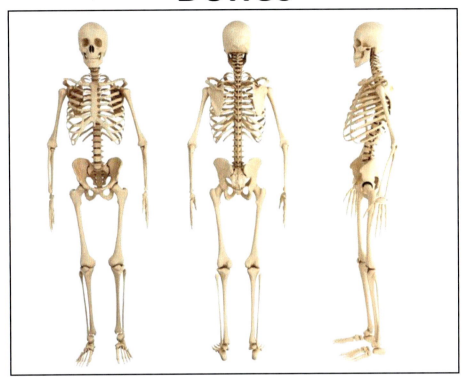

The bones of the human skeleton are strong

Teachable Truths:

The skeleton is made up of many strong bones to give our bodies the ability to live and function for over 75 and sometimes 90 years. By adulthood, we end up with 206 bones. The human skeletal system has five major functions- the production of blood cells (in marrow), for support, for movement, for protection, and for storage of minerals such as calcium. There are 26 bones in the human foot. The human hand and wrist contain 54 bones. The femur, or thighbone, is the longest and strongest

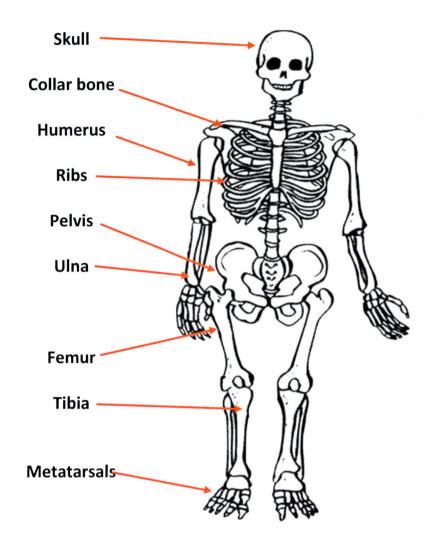

Color the bones of the human skeleton

bone of the human being. The stapes, in the middle ear, is the smallest and lightest bone of the human skeleton. If broken our bones will re-grow and repair themselves. Like our skin, the body's bones are also constantly being re-made, to the point where every seven years we essentially have new bones. Bones are held in place at joints by muscles and tissues called ligaments.

Verse to review:
Proverbs 17:22 A cheerful heart is good medicine, but a crushed spirit dries up the **bones**.

Take Home Points:

This proverb teaches us a straightforward principle. Being cheerful or happy is good for your health and having a "crushed" spirit or being sad about yourself or your situation is not healthy for you. Your spirit is your inward self which is made up of your emotions and your mind.

Happy is good

Sadness is hard

Real joy comes from knowing God on a personal basis, like a friend. What a friend we have in Jesus! We can talk with him through prayer. He helps you through hard times in life. Only he can give you a good self-image when others put you down.

When your mind is not right, your body can become ill. That is what "dry bones" means. Dry bones are useless and break like wooden splinters. Healthy bone has a strong marrow, where blood is produced. Blood flowing throughout the body is the life-giving liquid of a human being. Blood is a great gift from God.

Praying and reading the Bible is good

Reading the Bible will help you and make you strong. God's Word is truly the "Water of Life" so that your bones will never dry up! A cheerful person can choose to be happy even in difficult times. You can be a person who looks at the glass "half full" with water instead of "half empty." Learn to be content in your situation. Do not be a person with a negative attitude who complains about everything. (read **Philippians 2:14**) Having joy as a Christian is a command in the Bible. (read **Philippians 4:4**, 1

Thessalonians 5:16) We don't honor God by being a sourpuss all the time!

Sin can be destructive and crush your heart. Sin is anything that goes against God. Confess your sins to God, and repent. *Repent* means to change and live the way God wants you to live. It means turning away from sin. Ask God to help you to not sin and go against him!

Other key verses:
Philippians 2:14 Do everything without arguing or complaining.
Philippians 4:4 Rejoice in the Lord always; I will say it again, rejoice.
1 Thessalonians 5:16 Be joyful always!

Conclusion: Having a joyful attitude will help your health. Being sad leads to problems with one's physical well-being.

Ears

Our outer ear magnifies sounds to make them louder

Teachable Truths:

The ears allow us to hear, listen, and have good balance. The ear is divided into three parts – the outer ear, the middle ear, and the inner ear. The outer ear is the visible part of the ear and it directs the sound through an outer canal. This canal at times can be blocked with ear wax. The sound that enters the outer ear makes the eardrum vibrate. These vibrations are picked up by three bones called the stapes, malleus and the incus which form a

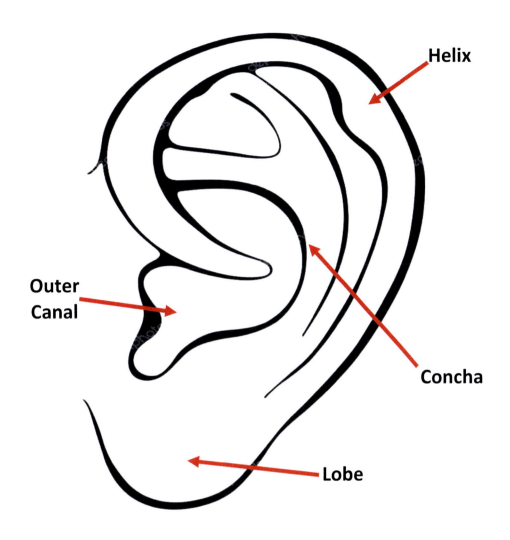

Color the ear your skin color

bridge in the middle ear. The stapes sends the vibrations to the oval window. Sound then gets amplified (louder). The sound moves into the inner ear called the 'labyrinth.' The inner ear has a small snail-like organ known as cochlea where the sound is changed into electrical impulses. These impulses are next sent to brain's auditory (hearing) center.

The middle chamber of the ear is also connected to the throat by a tube named the Eustachian tube. This tube strikes a balance between the body pressure and the pressure in our atmosphere.

Verse to review:
Proverbs 23:12 Apply your heart to instruction and your **ears** to words of knowledge.

Take Home Points:

Pay close attention to this proverb. Listening is an important virtue for all of us to pursue in our lives. (read **James 1:19-20**) To apply the instruction that you get from reading God's word, you must hear it first and then closely listen. The willingness to hear comes from a desire to learn. The knowledge in the Bible will help you to make right decisions. God in the book of **Hosea 4:6** says this, "My people are destroyed from a lack of knowledge." Faith is the cornerstone of being a Christian! Faith starts with *hearing* the word of Christ! (read **Romans 10:13**)

Focus on learning wisdom from the Bible and to apply its important principles to your life. What changes can you make today to honor God in all that you say and do? Learn the pearls of knowledge daily in the Word of God. Read, study, and meditate (focus) on it. Ask the Holy Spirit to guide you. (read **Revelation 2:7a**)

Other key verses:

James 1:19-20 Take note of this: Everyone should be quick to listen, slow to speak, and slow to become angry, for a person's anger does not bring about the righteous life that God desires.

Revelation 2:7a He who has an ear, let him hear what the Holy Spirit is saying.

Conclusion: Learn to be a good listener. Hear the Word of God as much as you can and apply it to your life.

Face

The face can make many different expressions

Teachable Truths:

Your face is unique and makes you who you are! It is made up of skin, muscles, 14 bones, the mouth, lips, nose, eyes, eyebrows, cheeks, forehead, and chin. Many of the muscles are directly connected to the skin on the face. Our ears and nose are made from a flexible tissue called cartilage. It takes 12 facial muscles to smile. We can make thousands of facial expressions. The six most common are: happy, sad, angry, disgusted, surprised, and afraid. True happiness is revealed in our eyes, true sadness is revealed in the muscles of our chin. The masseter muscle is the muscle we use to chew and is the strongest muscle in the human body. It can pull up to 80 times its own weight! Just like the rest of your body, if you exercise your facial muscles it will tone and firm them.

Color a face: eyes, ears, nose, mouth, hair

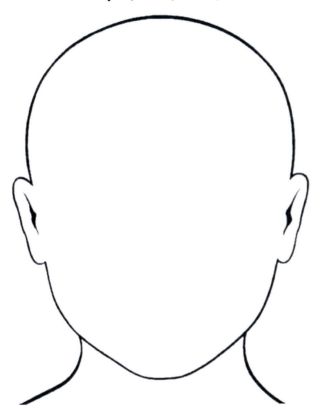

Cheeky dimples are inherited and are caused by shortened muscles. Lips are red because of the higher number of tiny capillaries that are just below our skins surface.

Verse to review:
Proverbs 27:19 As water reflects a face, so a person's heart reflects what's inside.

Take Home Points:
Water in a pond, calm lake, or peaceful river makes

a natural mirror. Looking into the water shows us an image of our face. Facial expressions can show surprise, happiness, anger, depression, anxiety, or hatred, to name a few. Our hearts are the same also. That is what this proverb is saying. Every person has emotions, imaginations, joys, and disappointments that are *similar*. God makes the hearts of all people alike (read **Psalm 33:15**), just like all races have similar bloodlines. (read **Acts 17:26**) Humans do not have the temperament of a bird, dog, or lion. That would be crazy!

These Vietnamese kids have happy faces

However, we can know ourselves better by watching other people. Though people are unique, they have similar desires and thoughts. It is pride that makes us think that we are better than others. We should learn how to be happy with those who are happy and cry with those who are crying. We can know how to treat others by how we want to be treated.

This is the golden rule taught by Jesus in **Luke 6:31**.

We know our hearts are capable of good, but this is only because of the *Holy Spirit who is working in us*. We need to learn how sin affects our hearts. The same heart can love or hate or be tempted. The same heart can be happy or sad. This should make us be able to forgive others because we are not perfect!

Jesus lived a life on Earth as a man. He was fully human and God at the same time. He grew up as a carpenter. He was tempted like we are, but never sinned.

Jesus with his mother Mary and father Joseph

He knew what physical and emotional pain felt like. He even died for us on a cross made of wood so that we might live forever. He can completely relate to us because he lived on earth *as a man*. That is what makes our personal relationship with him so special.

Other key verses:

Psalm 33:15 God forms the hearts of all people and knows everything that people think and do.

Acts 17:26 From one man (Adam), God made every nation of peoples, that they should inhabit the whole earth; and he determined the times set for them and the exact places where they should live.

Luke 6:31 Jesus said, "Do to others as you would have them do to you."

> **Conclusion**: Treat others like you want to be treated. Be compassionate to others.

Jesus's face shows his caring attitude for children and animals

Fingers

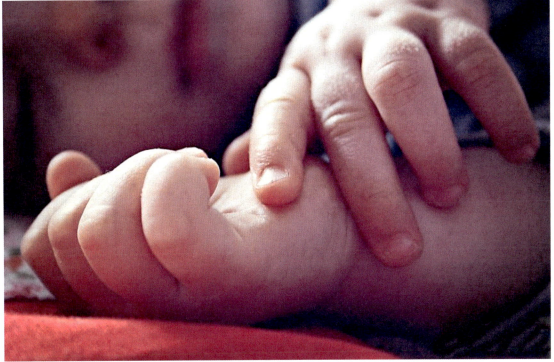

Ever think about why we have a total of 10 fingers?

Teachable Truths:

A human has five fingers on each hand. With our fingers we paint, play musical instruments, write, pull, grip, pluck, measure, and feel. The first digit is the thumb, after that, it is index, the third is center, the fourth is ring and the fifth is the tiny or pinky. Fingertips are extremely sensitive to temperature, texture, moisture, pressure, and vibration and send many messages to the brain by their nerves. Each hand has 29 major and minor bones, as well as 123 ligaments holding the whole

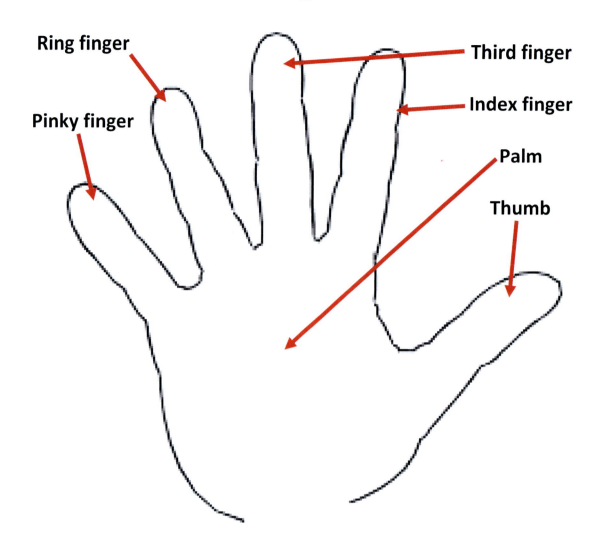

Color the hand and the fingers

structure together. Fingerprints are unique to every human being. Fingernails are made of the same material as hair. Studies show that children who have long fingers are better at math. Each finger has only one muscle, and it is called the arrector pili muscle. The man with the biggest hand in the world is Lui Hua of China. His index finger is about 12 inches long!

Verse to review:
Proverbs 7:3 Bind my commandments on your fingers so that you will live; write them on the tablet of your heart.

Take Home Points:

When I was a growing up, I learned to use my fingers sometimes when counting and found it helpful. If a teacher asked me a question and I did not know the answer right away, but almost, I would say, "The answer is right on my fingertips!" That is exactly how this proverb uses "fingers."

Solomon is not saying you should tie God's commandments on your fingers or write them on a stone tablet of your heart, but rather you should *know* them so well they are fixed in your mind. This way, you can live by right principles! We do this by meditating (or focusing) on God's Word and memorizing key verses. King David said this in **Psalm 119:11**: "I have God's Word in my heart so that I will not sin against him." Knowing God's ways in the Bible helps us to transform our minds away from the world's principles which are often against God. (read **Deuteronomy 6:6-7**, **Romans 12:2**) Living for

God is the best way to live!

There are many key lessons we should learn well, but the main ones are the ten commandments in **Exodus 20:3-17**. Here they are in basic terms: 1) Put God first in your life 2) Do not make any other gods in your life 3) Don't swear and take God's name in vain 4) Go to church regularly and have a day of rest to focus on God 5) Honor your parents 6) Don't murder 7) Be faithful to your husband or wife 8) Don't steal 9) Don't lie, and 10) Don't wish you had something your neighbor has. Learn to be content!

The Christian tries to follow God's principles. For example, look at this chart:

Commandments	The Christian	▲ An unbeliever
Puts God first	★	
Makes other gods		★
Doesn't mind swearing		★
Doesn't go to church		★
Honors their parents	★	
Doesn't murder	★	
Doesn't steal	★	
Lies regularly		★
Doesn't envy others	★	

▲ An unbeliever does not believe that God exists and does not obey his principles

Other key verses:

Deuteronomy 6:6-7 You must think constantly about these commandments that I, the Lord God, am giving to you. You must teach them to your children and talk about them when you are at home or out for a walk; at bedtime and the first thing in the morning.

Romans 12:2 Do not copy the behavior and customs of this world but be a new and different person with a fresh newness in all you do and think. Be transformed!

Conclusion: Commit to knowing God's principles so that your mind will be changed and you will be a new person.

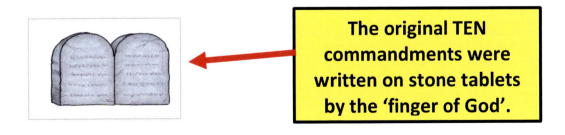

The original TEN commandments were written on stone tablets by the 'finger of God'.

Head

Our brain is like a computer

Teachable Truths:

The head of a human being contains an incredible computer called the brain. Our mind, thoughts, understanding, moods, calculations, memory, personality, will, and imagination come from our brains. The brain only weighs about three pounds and is ¾ water but is has over 85 million nerve cells called neurons which make up the gray matter. The brain has a split-second response time and that is about 1000 impulses per second, or 270 M.P.H. The brain of a two year old human is 80% the size of an adult brain. There are 400 miles of blood vessels in the brain. The brain is capable of 1,016 processes per second, which makes it far more powerful than any existing computer. Your brain's storage capacity is considered virtually unlimited. It does not get "used up" like RAM (memory) in your computer. The brain is contained in a super-hard bone called the skull, which is difficult to break. The head is also made up of the face, eyes, ears, nose, and mouth. Through the senses, these organs input messages into the brain.

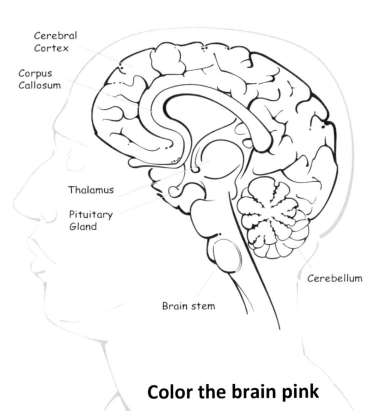

Color the brain pink

Verses to review:
Proverbs 25:21-22 If your enemy is hungry, give him food to eat; if he is thirsty, give him water to drink. In doing this, you will put a lot of burning coals on his **head**, and the Lord will reward you.

Take Home Points:

God thinks this proverb is so important it is continually taught over 1600 years by Moses in the Old Testament **Exodus 23:4-5**, and then Jesus in **Matthew 5:44**, and the apostle Paul in **Romans 12:20**. Read these verses for great insight. In ancient times, adding high heat to metal ore would cause the desired metals to melt and run free from the rest of the impurities. *Blazing coals* put on top of fire would increase the heat even more.

Blazing coals are "red hot"

Similarly, showing kindness to your enemy will often melt their hatred away for you. The head (which contains the mind and thoughts) of an enemy would be in shock about goodness showed to it by the Christian enemy. The intense heat may bring forth shame, repentance, and a desire for forgiveness. It shows how strong God's love really is.

The enemies talked about in these proverbs are not national enemies (like North Korea or the Communists if you are American) or enemies of the law (like murderers and thieves)! You certainly are not expected by God to love a murderer for the bad crime they have committed. For example, governments can go to war to protect their citizens, or they put the murderer in prison for justice.

This proverb is talking about *your neighbor next door, who may also be your enemy*. They may strongly dislike or curse you because you are a Christian. The story of the Good Samaritan defines a person's neighbor. (read **Luke 10:30-37**) The Jewish people and the Samaritans were enemies, but the Samaritan still helped the wounded Jew, when everyone else turned away.

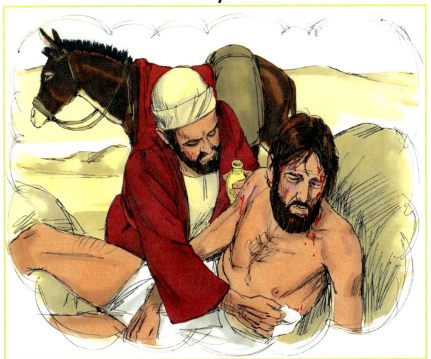

Jesus said we should copy the Good Samaritan. Your sinful nature and the thinking in your head go against this principle, but God's standard is high.

Other key verses:

Exodus 23:4-5 If you come upon an enemy's ox or donkey that has strayed away, you must take it back to its owner. If you see your enemy trying to get his donkey onto its feet beneath a heavy load, you must not go on by, but must help him.

Matthew 5:44 Jesus said, "But I say to you, love your enemies! Pray for those who persecute you!"

Romans 12:20 "If your enemy is hungry, feed him; if he is thirsty, give him something to drink. In doing this, you will heap burning coals on his head." Do not be overcome by evil but overcome evil with good."

Conclusion: Learn to love your enemy as you love yourself. Who is your enemy?

Stomach

Our stomach digests the food we eat

Teachable Truths:

Our stomach is in the upper abdomen (belly) near the ribs and starts food digestion. Digestion is the act of "breaking down food." Food is first chewed in the mouth and then swallowed through the esophagus tube where it then lands in the stomach. The stomach is a sac which moves food back and forth to allow it to be broken down into molecules our bodies can use. High concentrated acid is produced by the cells in the wall of the stomach which starts the breakdown of food. The stomach produces 3 quarts of this hydrochloric acid in a single day! It normally takes from four to six hours to digest one meal. The stomach is also important for our immune (defense) system. Hydrochloric acid in stomach kills bacteria and viruses entering with the food. Burping releases the air we intake with food. The stomach can hold up to half a gallon of food or liquid.

Verse to review:
Proverbs 13:25 The righteous eat to their hearts' content, but the **stomach** of the wicked goes hungry.

Take Home Points:

A doctor gives a prescription so we can get better when we are sick. This proverb gives us a prescription for a happy life. It gives us a lesson on God's control of our lives and about the importance of being content with what we have. To be content means *to be satisfied*. A person living right is someone who puts God first in their lives and makes

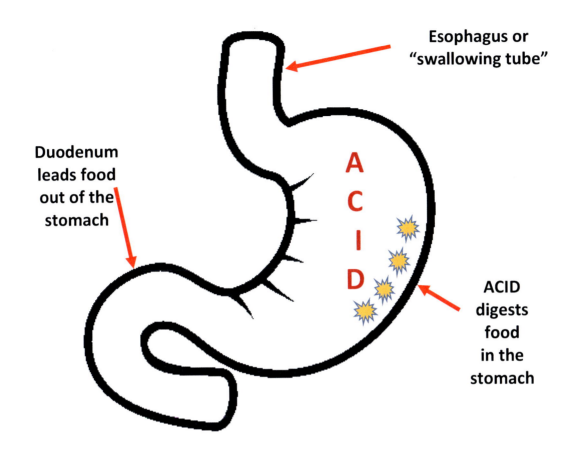

Color the stomach pink

godly, right choices. (read **1Timothy 6:6**) A satisfied person is happy and content with what they have been given from God.

The definition of 'wicked' in this proverb is *not choosing the godly way*. When we are not making choices God would want us to, we choose what the world chases after. The wicked want an excess of everything: money, food, entertainment, and power. They are never satisfied, and because of this are frustrated. They are always hungry for more. They are jealous of what other people have. Never being satisfied leads to being worried and depressed.

The 'righteous' person eats just enough to be satisfied. Whatever food or drink he, he is happy with it. The righteous individual chooses to be content. (read **Philippians 4:11**) Because his heart is happy in the Lord, no matter what food is on his table, he is satisfied. (read **Ecclesiastes 5:18**)

Other key verses:
1 Timothy 6:6 Godliness with contentment is great gain.
Philippians 4:11 The apostle Paul says, "I have learned to be content in whatever the circumstances."
Ecclesiastes 5:18 It is good and proper for a person to eat and drink and to find satisfaction in their work under the sun during the days of life that God has given them.

Conclusion: Learn to be thankful for what God has given you. Fill your heart with his Spirit and you will always be satisfied.

Teeth

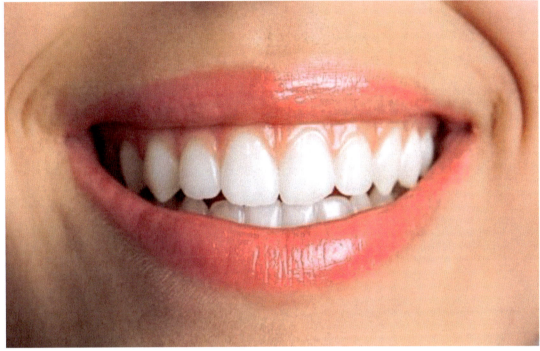

Our teeth help us to chew food

Teachable Truths:

Teeth start to form even before we are born—baby teeth start to form when the baby is in the womb, but they show when the child is between 6-12 months old. Humans have only two sets of teeth in their entire lifetime—baby teeth and permanent teeth. Enamel which covers our teeth is the hardest substance in the human body. The teeth are hard to be able to chew food for the 80,000 meals the average human has in a lifetime! Once we have our permanent teeth, we need to take good care of

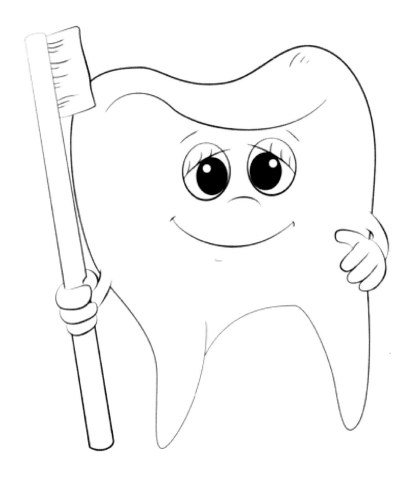

Color the tooth white and the brush red

them. One third of our teeth is underneath the gums—this means only two thirds of our tooth's length is visible. The average person spends almost 40 total days brushing their teeth over a lifetime. People who drink three or more glasses of soda each day have 62% more cavities than others. If you do not floss, you miss cleaning 40% of your tooth surfaces. Humans have 32 teeth, dogs have 42 teeth, cats have 30 teeth, pigs have 44 teeth, and an armadillo has 104 teeth!

Verse to review:
Proverbs 25:19 Like a bad **tooth** or a lame foot is relying on the unfaithful in times of trouble.

Take Home Points:

A bad tooth is one that has been damaged. Perhaps cracked by an accident or from chewing on something hard. The other problem might be an infected tooth. Either way, a bad tooth is usually very painful and not easy to live with unless it is fixed or removed. In the proverb, a 'lame' foot has been injured so that it has become useless.

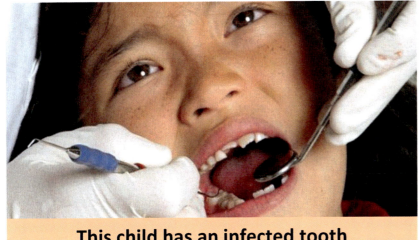
This child has an infected tooth

In this proverb, Solomon teaches us that relying on a friend who is not faithful to you is painful and useless because disappointment will likely follow. These friends might be by your side when things are going well, but sometimes when you need help, they will desert you. These friends are called "fair weather friends." Let's say you break an arm and

need help at school carrying your books around to different classrooms. A faithful friend will take the time to come to your rescue and help to carry your books!

Jesus is a faithful friend to us. He is always loyal. And he teaches us to be faithful and committed to him. Unfaithfulness is like a rotten tooth. It must be removed so you can be a healthy again. God is teaching us also not to put confidence in an unfaithful friend.

The Bible describes people who are unfaithful. They lack commitment. Peter, who was one of the twelve disciples and for a short while deserted Jesus. Judas, the treasurer of the disciples, betrayed Jesus also.

True friends are a great comfort to us. (Read **Ecclesiastes 4:9-10**.)

Other key verses:
Ecclesiastes 4:9-10 Two are better than one, because they have a good return for their work. If one falls, his friend can help him up.

Conclusion: Learn to be a faithful friend and more fully committed to God.

Some of Jesus' best friends were his disciples

Following God

If you want God to rule in your heart, here are the steps:

Through Jesus and the Holy Spirit, God will change your life! You will then make God first in your life and make him Lord of all your decisions. Parents and grandparents, you can walk your children and grandchildren through these steps below. **John 3:16** says "This is how much God loved the world: He gave his Son, his one and only Son. Why? So that no one need be destroyed; by believing in him, anyone can have a whole and everlasting life." This is a key verse in the Bible. The apostle Paul shared the Gospel, or the Good News for all humans, to us in the New Testament **1 Corinthians 15:3-7**. "The first thing I did was place before you what was placed so emphatically before me: that the Messiah died for our sins, exactly as Scripture tells it; that he was buried; that he was raised from death on the third day, again exactly as Scripture says; that he presented himself alive to Peter, then to his closest followers, and later to more than five hundred of his followers all at the same time, most of them still around (although a few have since died); that he then spent time with James and the rest of those he commissioned to represent him; and that he finally presented himself alive to me."

The Book of Romans in the New Testament can help you with four steps:

Step #1- We must all realize that we are sinners and that we need forgiveness. We are not worthy of God's grace. Right now, admit that you are a sinner, and need God. **Romans 3:23** "For all have sinned and fall short of the glory of God." That is, nobody deserves to go to heaven to be with Jesus on their own merit.
Step #2- Through Jesus, God gave us a way to be saved from our sins. God showed us his love by giving us the potential for life through the death of his Son, Jesus Christ. Do you believe this with all your heart? **Romans 5:8** "But God demonstrates his love toward us, in that, while we were still sinners, Christ died for us." An incredible act of grace and mercy.
Step #3- If we remain in sin, we will die and not go to heaven. However, if we accept Jesus as our Lord and Savior, and repent of our sins, we will have eternal life. **Romans 6:23** "For the deserved punishment of sin is death, but the free gift of God is eternal life in Christ Jesus our Lord."
Step #4- **Romans 10:9** "If you confess with your mouth the Lord Jesus and believe in your heart that God has raised Him from the dead (the resurrection), you will be saved and go to heaven *and* be saved from hell."

"Saved" means going to heaven forever. You can never be saved by trying to be a good person, nor can you be saved through any amount of 'doing good'. **Ephesians 2:8-9** says "For by grace have you been saved by faith. And that, not of yourselves. It is the gift of God, not of works. Lest any person should boast.

Proverbs in this Book

Proverbs 7:3 Bind my commandments on your **fingers** so that you will live; write them on the tablet of your heart.
Proverbs 13:25 The righteous eat to their hearts' content, but the **stomach** of the wicked goes hungry.
Proverbs 17:22 A cheerful heart is good medicine, but a crushed spirit dries up the **bones**.
Proverbs 23:12 Apply your heart to instruction and your **ears** to words of knowledge.
Proverbs 25:19 Like a bad **tooth** or a lame foot is relying on the unfaithful in times of trouble.
Proverbs 25:21-22 If your enemy is hungry, give him food to eat; if he is thirsty, give him water to drink. In doing this, you will put a lot of burning coals on his **head**, and the Lord will reward you.
Proverbs 27:19 As water reflects a **face**, so a person's heart reflects what is inside.
Proverbs 31:20 She (the wife of noble character) opens her **arms** to the poor and extends her hands to the needy.

Principles Taught in this Book

- Help the less fortunate
- Have a joyful attitude
- Be a good listener
- Hear the Word of God frequently
- Be compassionate
- Learn God's principles so you can be changed
- Love your enemy as yourself
- Be a faithful friend
- Learn to be thankful for what you have

Made in the USA
Columbia, SC
29 July 2021